D1262178

Praise for *My Pleasure*

"Irene Silt's My Pleasure tops from the underworld, where 'the inverse of pain / is in no way pleasure, it is acceptance.' Silt's poems wander straight into the throat of capital, purging loss in order to touch what we all must 'thrust aside / in order to live.' Desire spills out of Silt's mouth: jaw locked in exhaustion, where the trick and the lover blur in the direct address. Destroying time, rotting money, and leading us into the trenches of wanting, these poems are odes to the power of finding yourself flat on your back. Like the glow of a primal wound, Silt's poems teach us how to suffer—and how to love—more exquisitely."

— Rosie Stockton

"Irene asks, 'What if I am against boundaries?' and we are left with our limits. These poems bring us into the ecstatic tremors and absolute terror of self knowledge, all touch a violent mirror to the world and a flight line from the inflexible motions of capital. My Pleasure throws every possible angle of light upon desire so that we may see its shadow, honestly. What do we lose when wanting becomes having, when work becomes pleasure, when we are forced into the waning existence of escape? What do we win when we lose ourselves?"

— Nora Treatbaby

"We were being filmed as the twink rammed into me and my head hit the cheap tile wall of the fleabag motel's shower stall. There was something like an occlusion then, I worshiped his skin for the camera, and then my head hit the cheap tile wall again and again and so. I think of that sound as an evidence of what Catherine Clément would term syncope, an absence of self, and in Irene Silt's My Pleasure, the syncopic moment of rupture is ever-present. Silt's indelible book forms an argument that there is no stable subject—'the mulch fell away / in my arms was a large black snake'—but instead a porosity of subjectivity that is made most apparent in moments of fluidity, in fucking both as a means of survival and a means of battling hegemonic systems that attempt to master or explain every fissure, every tear. It also asks the questions, 'What might we want, when the wanting is finally able to dig in? What is deeper in life than just wanting to live?' And then the book answers itself: 'There is nothing in the world / to move a body but another body.' But do not be mistaken—Silt's is not a book about love, but instead a moving lyric treatise on the desire for liberation, a question about the boundaries of flesh and subject, and a positing that our desires are undefinable, as indefinite as ourselves, and as dynamic, like water. The book is sopping wet, dive in."

– Ted Rees

Praise for *The Tricking Hour*

"More than a polemic against work (though it is a very good one) The Tricking Hour is a meditation on what it means to process the world through your body; to feel life—love, loss, pain, ecstasy—to the fullest extent possible, all while knowing that your body is not (only) yours to control, that people with immense power get to dictate how you use your body, and thus how you experience the world. Silt writes compellingly about the issues facing sex workers, but their lessons about autonomy and pleasure under capitalism apply to all of us."

– P.E. Moskowitz

"These essays constitute a carefully and beautifully formed nebula of revolutionary thought and praxis. Silt's gorgeous synthesis is led by both righteous anger and gestures of deep care, born and fostered in spaces, booths, and backrooms both inconspicuous and flatly public. To encounter this missive is to encounter one of the truest manifestations of learning and living life past capital, past work's totaling reach, and into a life centered around love."

– Ryan Skrabalak

My Pleasure
By Irene Silt

DELUGE BOOKS

©Irene Silt, 2022
All rights reserved

Published by Deluge Books
info@delugebooks.com
New York / Los Angeles

Design and cover by Violet Office

ISBN: 978-1-7362104-7-5
Distributed by Ingram

private booth

I.

Come over tonight
I will meet you at the door
Close it, let you in
like I hadn't planned it
A lure unlike the drive
nonbelief of satiation
I could fold over
Fold inside, anxiety in the
signs, mixed messages

You can't see it? Not even
under the skirt of dim light?

Pants and socks come
off in the same motion
Better than the physical
presence of a higher being
takes me here puts me
here and keeps me here
longer than you could
ever imagine as time at all

I am about you in that
you spill out of my mouth
In the silences and the avoidance
Rewrote every opportunity
Made it tragic
All my money smells rotten
Old like the air it's kept in
Each time I pay I smell
Smell all the times I didn't

Flushed, seemingly forever
Saw myself in the dirt
under my fingernails
Is that what we are calling it?
Swelling tumor,
function of possibility

What I thrust aside
in order to live
The embodiment of
ambivalence
I continue, assumed,
incommensurable

II.

Brought you to all the shores of all
the water, tried to triangulate my
memories through you. How I made
shape of the crescent from the window
to the bank to the parking garage

Did I know I could want so
patiently? Did I know the wanting
is my big song and dance, the one
you keep asking me to sing?

I am afraid to be done with any
thing. It'll be there when you
need, get it done, just get here

Each night working at a loss, more
full as I hollow out. The warmth of
inflammation, of chilled shot. Took
his pistol out of his pocket, laid it
down on the table, among the liquid
rings of ghosted drinks

Did you think I would let you up now?
I've let you hold me down, neck folded
on a wall, nothing sexy. Had to reckon
with abuse that keeps me childlike, biting
myself. My reversal technique is good and
clean but I haven't tried on you. Want the
beauty to be seen in the foreground, larger
element than speed. Wrote the devastation
off, sent the money order, it's taken care of

Stowed you away like that, perspiring
saliva from the nicotine withdrawal
Drank the water from the bottle filled
with ashes, never puked, just held it in

Pieces of leather flake off the couch, unreal
but gets the point across. Attractive if you
let it be, makes the most of the light. Got the
most out of the hour, ignored the hum of
a loose cord. I was late to all reference,
everyone's resilience filled me in

III.

Started to well up as I fit inside you
Made to be seen on the outside
facing as if I can't look with my hand
Cover my face, stick to it. Or you'll
hit yourself as they hit you
Only have to learn that once

Said you liked the taste, like bones
Brought it to you everyday
Ate radishes for the zinc
Metallic taste, like blood, like flesh
Ate more while you were away

They don't have what we have
Long limbs so we circle,
unable to take each other down
Speaking in the clench, in the hand fight
Get your grip make it happen again or
it's not gonna happen

Brought you to that tree so old makes you
feel closer to anything near your age. Any
thing from the past couple hundred years

That harrowing sound, hard to accept
Lions roaring from behind the fence
Only know because we heard them. An
anguish you'd think you only dreamt of

Now I will move all my objects closer to you
Painful is the cunt, hurts most of the time
Hurts to want hurts to not want
The outside is stretching in anticipation
Starts to creep in, dry when it can't get filled
Or overflows, begins so wet it gives me away
Gives me a sense of readiness I decided to have
decided one day and that was it

IV.

What if I am against boundaries
Reactionary proof you could seep in
Touch every part of me I cannot
reach Disgust me Send me packing
You got off as I stuffed my bag
Turned you on with a purpose
I am not a separation I am a chaining together
malleable signification
threat of open and wild
tame and closed

Wasteland predicates existence
Rendered invisible until you stepped in
Dumpsite and home
Someone will come take me away
WE BUY HOUSES FOR CASH
Yes I am ambiguous Yes I am hard to reach
Careful with your arm out there
I spit on the seepage I spit on myself

I am only a woman out of convenience
So close to the place which permits me to be
I remove myself from the arena of facts
You came to me for my rugged isolation
but I am the site of industry
We can do anything we want
Cut off a mountaintop for money
Remain sure of what I am, clean
Lose all interface with the world
What you are asking after is hearsay
Can't bring myself to repeat it
When I am not driving I am asleep
Look you in your eyes cause I know you want it

Irreconcilable harshness
rather look you in the mouth
listen to the feedback
Through the static realize
we just don't get along
Pungent smell begs me to return
Smeared on my bedsheets
Go to face it but I know better
If you control the head
you control the body

The solution is always to fuck
Let me be a reminder
I have asked how do I get out?
all the while I was trying to get in

V.

this is a face you reserve for me
behind your hair a private booth
a light remains turned on
I undo my own belt

there is a pure static
slight in-between
one finger strokes the edges
exchanges of grease

that anticipatory dissolve
sleepy from the delay, the downward
explain to me your good needs
let me forget who I am with my tongue

these margins of error
the mattress and the wall
give me back our beginning
I will let you win

my pleasure

I started to say my pleasure in response to
thank you
washing everyone's dishes
my pleasure
massaging the shoulder of a friend
my pleasure
driving us for hours through the night
filling up your glass stealing you that shit
developing your thoughts choking the dude out
my pleasure

everything made into pleasure

I have all this wetness that you don't have
and you come back at me with
you've got a way with words, use them
I plead, like, there are no words right now!
That would be my true pleasure, wordlessness

I speak for a lot longer in languages
you do not understand
I have desexualized everything but the room
You fooled yourself into thinking

I would unfold if you shook me hard enough

One time you really got me talking you said,
I should give you amphetamine salts more often
Looking at you, I picked up another armful of mulch
and it began to move. As I stood up, the mulch fell away
in my arms was a large black snake, cold
It unraveled and poured out of my arms as we gasped

What like, I am not aware of how I am fucking oozing??
That overcompensating solidity that is still so slick
Try to wash myself off myself. I become lost to air.

Blame it on the revolving door of my bed
or how the neglect made me masochistic
in a solitary way: a workaholic. There's an idea
of feminism as living with consequence,
lacerated bodies communicating their lacerated lives

Your cunt is hard to get to
It clamps down so fucking hard
and the one thing I did say is
I don't care for biting

My love of the below my love
of your self loathing which I inherited
To enter below we went to the attic
I stepped on the stain and took her photograph
She's wearing the t-shirt with faces and blood
I would prefer that our bodies be trapped here

My loss knows the pain of lying down
of being laid out, craving below
Broken noses on a door frame

Being washed out and hung up
Saying, *I would need so much out of you*
it is not even worth getting into
but then we will just continuously get into it over time

I am so angry at you, I would save your life
I would force you to live again, without me

You gave me a complex. You gave me
the utter certainty that the ways
of the underworld are perfect

When I was fisting you
I rested my arm on top of the A/C window unit
that time you were kneeling over me
my legs fell asleep
I gave them permission to float away

I pointed out that you always wear your underwear
backwards, the face you gave me was dirty
Often I am extremely rigid yet balled up,
I used to call myself a 2x4 but now I am like
crumpled steel. Often you say,
I can't tell if you want this
I cannot always tell myself
Pleasure is somewhere outside
the known and unknown
It is unknowingness, without any expectation
that one day it will become fact. It is the honesty
of me not knowing if I want your mouth
on me at all and the lack of expectation
that I will orchestrate your desire
That I will open up onto you
when there is no denying
this will be for our use

I keep thinking about you dancing
and your wavy arms in the corner of my eyes
I tried to get you alone a few times but gave up so easily
You called me your mirror hand and nothing rang as true,
compelling in a way we could only be to ourselves

You shared your vision of a velvet bedroom. I have almost offered many times to come help you staple it all over your walls. Is that what you want? So many of our desires are simple. They are within reach. What are your most unachievable desires, and what is desire in a world after achievement? What might we want, when the wanting is finally able to dig in? What is deeper in life than just wanting to live? I ask for practical reasons. If Marx himself was a whore, I think they would ask him what they ask me at the end of everything. What is sex without capital?

What is fucking when we are not fucking before work, or at work, or after work, or to get work. Not fucking as work or to make a child or to break a family or to lock you down. Not fucking to give something up or to give in or as a given. Not out of boredom or as our only thrill, or to convince someone of something. Not fucking as measure, or data, or study. Not to know what you could get away with or how far you can get, not because you are owed. Not in exchange for a bed. Or a house, or a meal. Or all your meals. All the unbroken parts of your body. Not for protection, not for stability, not for a passage.

My birth relegated me
to floating appendage
of my mother. Maneuvering
her body, understanding
her pleasures and her
pains, watching the ways
she medicated herself
The degradation of her body
and the fate of mine. I revel
in that and I make a living of it.

Maybe what approximates a liberating sexual encounter
is the time I was hit by a car. My physical therapist strapped
himself to me, moved his hips as a way to move my hips
I was confused by my own emotional response and you said to me
baby it's a role reversal. You were jealous of my exhilaration
my attachment and my personal growth. The bliss of a release
that made me feel lost outside the physical therapy dungeon

I have a body collision mode
from a lifetime of pressing up
against varied figures for varying
periods in various rooms, chairs
and booths, underneath sinks,
in back seats, where I can extract
pleasure from almost any situation

I can make you feel
exactly how you want to feel
and I can always make myself come
but I wouldn't do that to you

I am sorry I missed your DJ set tonight
Imagine a parallel world where I show up
nonchalant after refusing so many times, dance
with that nondescript face and my arms
sort of winding sort of shifting
through things. Instead I am here thinking
about how you are a gift to the world
About violence, boredom, and softness
I know you would like me to touch you more
but you don't know how healing
it is to really want to touch someone
The moment after refusal where you give in
has taught me that the inverse of pain
is in no way pleasure, it is acceptance

I am also thinking about the pleasure
of reading aloud to you, about the moment
before your sleeping medication sinks in
when coming is not enough release
I am thinking about how long I continue
after I feel you deep asleep on my chest.

I am your right appendage your left appendage
Where are you now and where
do you need to be to do what you need to do?
Sex will be something we do together
to do everything else we need to do in the world

Your mouth is naturally a pout
When you say the most interesting things
you tilt your head up and all I see is a deep frown
My mouth immediately takes the same shape

When we were having sex you started to cry
wrapped up in it all I was so wrapped up in you
I didn't even pause. The effortless mixture.

A few nights later with the LSD, the poppers,
the Sade and the linen, the purple light, the sweat
and the Key of Dreams, the remarkable swirl
Not thinking about your tendency for over stimulation
or what you might like or not like. When your body was not
a problem to solve but a mesmerizing immersion
In my head over and over, can I come inside you
is it ok if I come inside of you? I came inside myself.

The hottest week of the year is my
inability to consume, or how you
cannot fit entirely inside of me. It is like
kissing, but smearing. To smash together
so that we may be indistinguishable,
feel we are soft right now, cherish that,
know of the vital strength still held
in the fading firmness encapsulating our bodies

My memories of having sex with her
are all made up. Don't come by,
it's been a long day, I would want
to lie about it after

Availability is not really a question
but it's a nice way to put it
I am here in the room to be fucked
There are three blacklist entries
under this name. He asked
many times how I ensure my safety,
how do you know who you can trust?

Now it is the middle of the night,
there are noises in the hallway or
another room. Something violent,
unconsensual sex, men yelling
about that ass, moans or maybe
my head replaying my own moans
My own moans that often sound
like they are in the hallway
or another room

Risk analysis has made my cunt
into an algorithm. They describe me
as sensual but I am not so sure
they call me passionate

Pleasure might rot if it is not rinsed off
We let it fester and fill up so that
we can extract substance from it

Pleasure would leave the earth
if it wasn't the earth itself
I would let it go in peace

Pleasure could be nothing and we fuck it up
by making it something to be had. My pleasure
has echoed, alone in the space behind that
wall I cannot see without a mirror

I realize what I've been doing,
how it has compounded
Whores are the destroyers of time
in that we are deeper than time
nothing has time, yet we
have captured it.

The best thing she said to me was
you are in this entirely by yourself
it's just you, alone in that room

I am disgusted by the sounds
of mouths against themselves
I feel the impossibility of filling
each pothole left open by each flood
All the softness of bodies has hardened
You think I do not want any of your mush
I have been here with my mouth open
and now it is dry

I walked into your room
and sat down with you on the floor
It was the same spot where we fucked
to Motörhead six months ago, hot, thick, and dirty
You still make me come every time

Your face feels like clay. My fingers
smear over your lips up your cheek
down your nose, I am molding it myself
It ends up exactly how I want it

We could make something like love
to remediate the sharp, dry air surrounding us
The sweat from our bodies would humidify
the air back to the weight it was when
we fucked right here and fell asleep

I heard you wailing through the window
I tried to open your door, but I had locked it behind me

Promises, Promises was playing in the bar
I wanted for a more ambiguous breakup
melancholic but not sad, still throbbing
You never left enough space for me to
saunter back. The luxurious agency
of regret and second chances

I pulled the sheet over both of our heads
and I looked at you even though it was
difficult. Eventually I brought you toward me
kissed you deeply. You waited for me to do it,
I let you swallow your apology

It is horrible to be reminded of what you miss
by what you miss itself. To hold it in front of
your face and pull it toward your mouth
I am watching her breathe me in. Love is
preservation and pleasure could be accumulating
things then breaking them down

Your presence fills me up, it is like
sludge. When you leave it is slow
and stubborn to drain

In my head before I see you I practice saying
I need you to hit me with a closed hand
This is not exclusive to you but it is specific
My pleasure is contained yet diffuse like a landfill,
its reach is unknown though you have symptoms
You are very sweet to dig me out but I am still a cave

Once you suggested that I take you out of the equation
This made me want to spit in your mouth
I have exquisite thoughts about you,
they are addressed to my own body
Yours is worthy of adornment
though your skin already glows

My nails began to hurt you after you finished
There is a certain outward force which alleviates
pain but it is a fine line. Awake in my cell I replayed
the scooter smashing into the window of the bank
I figure if I concentrate hard enough, I could be
the object thrown against what we want to destroy

I am not motivated by sex
but to smash. Press up against
something not quite me. To connect in order
to understand the promises of control
and fabrication, of the return. My body
left behind as the cop kneels on my back

The only statement I have arrived at is
everything feels mixed up. There is an honest
struggle and it is met with the most flowing
entanglement of arms. I am bound by myself,
pressed to crush you on top of me. So obsessed
with your body it feels smaller than I remember
every time. How do you weigh me down more
than myself? Enter my thoughts like warm water,
like embarrassment, the flood after a sharp pain
I let you go farther and you become more radiant
In my head I tell you, there is nothing you couldn't
do to me. I will take a broken jaw, don't hold back

I can feel my insides surround
me. I try to open my eyes but they
stick to themselves. I am not ready
to see it for myself

When you fuck me I entirely decompose
It is this solvency that leaves us without
words. Early on we had to talk about it all
more often. I can't remember the order of
things. I borrowed the car and when I returned
she sobbed in my arms half asleep

Inside deeper skid and slap, we fucked
in silence and tears came to my eyes
All the ways I have looked onto you,
the blood starts to return

My most distinct memory is the fire
reflecting in your eyes framed by my
white t-shirt wrapped around your face

There is nothing in the world
to move a body but another body

You said money only exists for
the irreconcilable, when two things are
of different value and we cannot find
any other way to settle up. This will
be clear when he says, *I know you are
submissive because you listen. When I
pull your hair you tilt your head back.
If I give you a thousand dollars, there
will be no limits.*

Pleasure is not free while we
stand on top of it. I have seen it
ripped away like a tattered rug
The entire room is the air between
your curls. Soft, floating, abundant
The pink light which is generous,
hides the edges and the source,
smooths us over

How will we get here again?
How do I get it both harder
and less? Being pleased is
very different than getting
what you asked for

Technique is never made
better through force. There
are things you can do. Make
it more beautiful, do it faster
but the pain is always there
the pain will always come

I worked so hard to get you off. Your quiet
yet brute moans were more satisfying than
the hourly rate. I had already calculated
everyone's cut. The smell of our cunts,
your sweater, my armpit, all undeniably real,
ripe, and previously worn. I held you like a
blanket in my lap. My hand was hot from
rubbing, you continued to moan in your sleep

Your husband grabbed me and looked me
in the eye. *I want you to push her limits.*
Men will attempt to move your hands
for you. You walked away and curled up
on the other couch. I enviously watched
you sleep for the remainder of the hour

Mediated pleasure is a messy pile
I am stacking up affairs until they
fall over and make themselves
known again in the wreckage

Unmediated pleasure
folds into itself. When
we made love in our friend's
yard a spider bit me over
and over in the same spot
I backed away from it when
I should have added pressure
With you I was relentless,
made sure you came twice

You called me at 7 in the morning. I was
in bed with someone else. You reminded me
who you were though your voice was familiar
It had obviously taken courage to call
The last time we talked you were full of shame
but now you sound like gratitude. Later I
remembered the magic. I read instructions
in a book then fucked you on the floor
inside of a candlelit pentagram in my apartment
positioned in the center of another pentagram
formed by the cemeteries in our small town
I said, envision your life five years from now
What do you want?

When we were on the way to bury your dad
I was taken by the blinking tail lights rolling
in a line through the hills. That weekend
all measure had fallen away. The sky
remained gray and the light bland
Your girlfriend asked me about
Catholic death rituals. I don't have
much to say though I have been to many
She has a beautiful way of talking,
a slow way of imparting knowledge
like folklore or family recipes

She described to me the death rituals
of Buddhism. The removal of entrails,
everything but the heart. Bodies stuffed
with wads of linen, sand, sawdust
I wanted that so badly my stomach churned
Stuff me with rosemary, the ashes of my friends,
teargas soaked bandanas, balaclavas and bombs
Ask around about where to leave me.

five poems

my decisions in the bathing water

Stillness is easy to appropriate
I can claim silence with a flag
Money showers pool
Into a stagnant puddle
I lap it up, taste your voice

Keep in mind I want you
I like to sit in front of it
Hold on and pretend it is mine
Protected by the doing
Feel it fill into my mouthful

No I do not think you are prude
Here, a locker room of encounter
A glide by, flash of your gap
Could it be the middle of you
Where I am lucky to know?

I heard you in my tonal *yeah*
The corner and the bottom
Open the centerfold as a hand
Never over watered not under sunned
The plant is rigid and taut

throw it away i don't need it

Salt will take off the last pounds
The first step is only to move on
fresh carpet and toes under plastic
See them fall in the unearthing

I found my branch and I sat there
Put the breath into my breath
Expose it long behind a curtain
My lips an edge made by light

Take me on as a reflective burden
Outline the parameters by ritual test
The plan was to work with my body
I would no longer need to try and piss

In that muffled and wanting voice
Would you say there is something
I wait like this on top of it
I am the brick in my own door

is it not internal

No idea of this hair that covers
Your asshole like a sand timer
It has named the presence of love
While we assumed its absence

Moments of underperformance
Side note of lust and dominance
It comes through my mouth
This growl, my stomach

I have woken up and ached
Anticipated sex in detachment
I could claim to have what you want
It is on its way back from the lab

Know that the day will end
Four different kinds of mush
Dissolve whole inside my mouth
It is the room which holds me up

naturally rigid

I had undone a compulsive form
Of motion the way it must be
Rubbed stiff against a soft plane

I will get off precisely on bone
Couched in latent aliveness
Passive existence of organ

Laid out calmly before me
There for us to know
I don't want to explain it

The birds echo in the courtyard
What made them that way
All at once

sick with a love for punishment

The patient wait
I am born of it

No laws on my mind
Nothing but surface

I tell the truth
It is mine to tell

Feel my come loom
Behind your back

Imagine it without me
I will be your hand

Unspoken tactile thrust
The steam engulfs my eyes

My body's final task
Disappears to itself

the noise commonly referred to as silence

I.

You stand and breathe heavily from motion I am irregular and distal. No want to be measured, tried to sneak it all by. The body is an instrument of perception I was encouraged to honor the ways it hurts itself. As if it is all an alarm, protective and more present than I would be honest to myself. The final coat of paint is drying. Eventually it will chip off. Blood flow is key here, flows downward, below my hips. Hover over the gap, let the non existent parts of me enter you. We don't have to be wet but we always are. Horrible noises if you really listen. Property can be lent out. See how long she lets me use it, catch the cum before it hits the bed. I know these are fresh sheets.

II.

I must be good to be alone with. More comforting than the glow of the TV. Carbonation hurts so you let it flatten, settle outside of your body. You want to feel me inside of you, become non separate, but what about the room? The strain of appliances. I can hear what keeps me, alive, malnourished, disgusted. You must make the distinction of your own body. I am grateful to be here in death. Throbbing light. I can see my vein twitching.

III.

Now it is in rotation, rubbing, unlike a heartbeat yet rhythmic. Can you give me time? Can you let me linger in the before? This zone of predetermination before I need any appendage. Before you walk, or stand, or sit. One overshot motion, a pirouette to the floor. Protect the head, the elongated spine. Gentle hand a reminder. I am yours but you are not mine. Beyond this periphery, scent. Your rotting scent I must have seen coming. I conditioned my whole life for this. I have trained for this perfection of love, the commitment that leads itself. Departs from asking permission. I have visions though the fear is contrived. It is the tether to the sewer. Crying out because you forgot where your voice comes from, your gut. You don't care about the dirt so much anymore but you'll light a candle. To fall, to flail, what else, to kneel. Kneel to pretend you know how to lift from your legs.

IV.

I have burned my hand exactly where my pen lays. My denial ran out, stunned into relaxation, that is my auditory gap. You've grabbed me back there, my pleasure lands ambiguous. Calmed movement, to feed. Nice to have it done to me. Do not speak to me with your shame. Tease me with your unease. All my distractions, personalized. Desire gaming you. Here, while you pee, I have finally relaxed. No I'm not into urine I am holding my own dick and hearing what I'd expect to hear. Took you in with me. I do look down at it. It's a sensitive area and I don't want to slow down in the name of accuracy. Working at a faster pace, to defeat various barriers at the same time. An opponent is most effectively submitted through exhaustion, burnout. They will be waiting to give in. You will say please. You will want it.

V.

The moan. Not even a death rattle you are so alive calling for help. I fumble before your misery. Skimming the ever-apparent surface of the body you can't move. When you do move, it is to comfort me. Spread to dismiss me from my duties. I only understand you as myself, each of us interprets your lack as our worst fears. I am struggling. I am becoming mean. Hotly desirable make her beg for forgiveness. Pumps and monitors. We are building something here. It is evident in the intensity, the stakes, explanations drawn out of why I can't at all. Love forgets paths. Windows are nice. I leave it open but only for the air, the street echo, inner shaft. I go out the door. I am traditional.

VI.

I want to take frugality back up. I have stopped all response, forgot about to do lists. Wrote the groceries in a line like this like prose. Going though the motions is good when you get paid. I see the exploit of the salary and expectations of free form thought and being. We lose a bit, loose energy from living, carry the motions to the bed of your mind, the couch, the bathtub, the hotel. My mother's bed. In my mind the room, the atmospheric overtones of what has been decided. What we are here for, drafted to do and be, our assignment. Grade me.

VII.

I prefer this cornered-off place. I see it but you can't because it is yours to offer up, velvet rope, pad lock. Plexiglass. Broom closet. Keep me there all night. Exhaust me.

VIII.

When I freeze you will have to decide whether to keep going. Baby I thought you were right behind me I thought you saw my opening, your ass sweeter than your mouth. I do try to accept the scent of your rotting tooth.

IX.

You are better than most in surprising ways. I had sounded it out. Weighed out time and crushed it into a line, flat. Bruised bone is what you want. Lasting and acute. I convinced you to do it. Behind my face, a bathroom stall. I can integrate your motive then leave you alone in your plan. Went back to fail mine. A fool for it. The lights are loud and it feels a long time. Don't you hear me moving? The sheet, the lamp, the overhead light. I am mean in my head, I like the sluts for that reason, they won't be overpowered. My commitment a way to put things off.

X.

I like to lay silent on top of you. I know you feel the volume, we are of similar mass. Think about how I have redistributed mine. Writhing, gliding, swimming. It's just humping. It is so goddamn horny too funny to do in the daylight, unless we are half clothed, or mad but not for real. I avoid make-up sex because arguments are already motivated by something. My response to this stare is without affirmation. Shame unwelcome. Kicks you out for that. I'm not up for it.

you

I might not have anything left to say about her. Maybe there is no importance, that I just have nothing left and she is a good thief. I still get sick at the thought of her body, as my mind believes fully that she is my own body. It is similar to when I see my mother's foot, deep red and purple, my stomach turns so intensely that time stops until I can be in my own head again instead of deep into my mother's body, a shared body I need to forget.

It is a sickness from longing. It is a sickness from wanting to be all of these people in my life, as in I want them as my own body while simultaneously sitting across from them or picking them up at the bus station or feeling the inside of them. I want the sensation of them as me and to see them in the non-place of the mirror. Something else but still devastatingly myself.

I want to touch another body so when I touch myself I can feel the difference. So when I try to recall an other, I can feel alone and dream in my head all the ways I could describe what it is for me to be away from them.

I am obsessed with them in my own interrogation of self, to leave myself behind, the self-reflective nature. It was not my own face that taught me the things I desire and am good at. I cannot explain that you are me so I have mostly left you alone, losing you. When I move through the many lives that appeared out of sneaking around with you, I found the right distance to scatter myself. Not dependent on being myself, the unrequited love affair is also distanced from ownership and sameness, never carried out or complete. I think behind and it starts back up again, I experiment.

Writing on you has allowed the return to a site. I rests into you, falls asleep and leaves the earth. I have understood something about the placement of my body specifically in relation to her, the ground. Skin surrounds me as a surface. It is a false barrier. It is made up of the inside, my internal. I look contained though I am losing heat, I let go before I decide to do so. All that I am proximal to. If I can disperse myself into this pile of you, this site I have called you, I will land in the past so that I may love it. That I may continue that truth alongside the horror that is also true. I believed it was hidden when really I just hadn't asked after you. I let you kind of breeze though without expectations, let you do and be you.

It had been so long since I heard from you. I had spoken out loud to you by mistake several times. When I read your message, I thought I was excited when really, a large daddy long legs was crawling across my arm. I needed that sensation to know that presence means more than being heard and to know I cannot claim to ever see your presence.

Here I have written about her in the return. I have gone back into her in my relentless way, without being prompted. I do away with any separation. I am still that encounter. New, fresh everyday.

You has never been a stand in. It is a vessel which holds and destroys us. When in love I wanted to know everything. Wild swath of your lies and the not-quite-evident. What I make you. My ultimate seduction is the acquisition of the knowledge I would like to help you find. Now it is through and I want for nothing. I do not look after a discrete period of feeling. The expansiveness is there as I look back and forward. But here I have finished and I would hate to understand. I refuse to distill reason from it. I don't need to know who it was back there in the floating world, indistinguishable in its memory, everything and nothing.

I cultivate a life of acceptance that both are true, that I left beauty behind and also it is still there. I know both modes at once. I forget nothing yet I do not recall in order to prove.

There is a limit to me. In order to escape totality I refuse to be a part of fate. This would be horrible, our relation a random twist. I also do not want to be part of now, where there is only self contained individuality. You were not given to me like a gift. I worked. I abducted you.

I placed you in my life, saw everything take shape to you, or I filled in the holes with insulation foam sealant. Hard billows, a grotesque archive in my mind of the time I say, I am going home. You can come with me if you want.

I am quite far from our activity. Though its facticity is there. It is fixed on the walls I know so well, as I spot painted every stain. The room slowly emptied out, the last thing we did was break a window.

We went in so far it is not possible to come back, we let the time pass in that way where everyone is gone without you noticing. We will not be spit back out to start over. Walk to the front of the bar from the bathroom in the back and the lights are on and you hear the birds.

You will look in the other direction and see everything has carried over, the signs and songs on repeat. There is an unplugged fan rotating in the window. I long for the feeling of circulating air with or without you.

Our relation called others into existence. I continue my time with my other lovers all of which caught their own true internal. I would never say you are different or more. I only know you exists because I wake up and I want for existence. Want for the sickness of continuing on after what was already found.

You found it so you look for yourself everywhere. A third thing now has meaning. I oscillate from being the light to standing in its rays. This detached perceptual mode becomes an equal force in my life to love. I is no longer dependent on being or submitted to an act. You are there. I am free.

ACKNOWLEDGEMENTS

I began writing *My Pleasure* in a workshop with Dawn Lundy Martin. It was further brought along in workshops with Anne Boyer, CA Conrad, Fred Moten, and Jackie Wang. Thank you to Precious Okoyomon for organizing these workshops as part of The Home School in 2019. "Private Booth" was written during a workshop with Ted Rees. Thank you, Ted, for opening me up. Thank you to Eric Sneathen, Melissa Mack, Allison Chomet, Tessa Micaela, Amy Sisson, and Chip Chapin for doing this with me. The entire manuscript of *My Pleasure* was brought to completion in a second workshop with Ted, and I am further grateful for the inspiration and continued collaboration of this group—Ryan Skrabalak, Alina Pleskova, Susannah Simpson, Phoebe Glick, and Ariel Yelen.

Thank you, KO'S, for continuing to partner with me in thought. Thank you to Sycamore and everyone who loves this place, where much of the book was written. Thank you to Laura for my home in Brooklyn where this book was finished. Thank you to my sister. Thank you Matt for your unwavering and loving perspective, which pushes my visions along. Thank you to my comrades, who are by no coincidence poets—Nora, Rosie, Mia, Slee, Jami, Cassandra, Kat, Sophie, Sarah, Coco, Dianna, Mal, Rona, Devin, Tom, Lotte, Yoann, Hunter, Ben, Rose, and Bella. Thank you to everyone who has gotten me out of jail over the years, especially my mother. Thank you to Willa, whose love makes possible more love.

Thank you to Deluge, for inviting me to share two books. I am grateful to Emily, Cyrus, Hannah, Beau, Phoebe, and Violet Office for bringing this book further than I could have imagined myself.

Fragments of the poem "My Pleasure" appear in *Poesis Journal.*

"Private Booth" was first published in *Spoil 2.*

Four of the "five poems" were first published in *LESTE #12.*

BIO

Irene Silt writes about power, anti-work feeling, joy, and deviance. Their essays and poems have been published in *Mask Magazine*, *ANTIGRAVITY*, *Spoil*, *LESTE*, *Trou Noir*, *Poiesis Journal* and in the *Tripwire* pamphlet series. They live in New York.

Also From Deluge Books

Mercury Retrograde
A Novel by Emily Segal

Black Venus Fly Trap
Poems by Jeanetta Rich

Amor Cringe
Fiction by K Allado-McDowell

The Tricking Hour
Essays by Irene Silt

delugebooks.com

CPSIA information can be obtained
at www.ICGtesting.com
Printed in the USA
JSHW022256250922
30833JS00004B/25

9 781736 210475